* Smithsonian

PROTEST MOVEMENTS

THEN AND NOW

BY ERIC BRAUN

CONSULTANT:
CHRISTOPHER WILSON
DIRECTOR OF EXPERIENCE DESIGN
NATIONAL MUSEUM OF AMERICAN HISTORY

CAPSTONE PRESS
a capstone imprint

Smithsonian is published by Capstone Press,
1710 Roe Crest Drive, North Mankato, Minnesota 56003
www.mycapstone.com

Library of Congress Cataloging-in-Publication Data Names: Braun, Eric, 1971- author.
Title: Protest movements : then and now / by Eric Braun Description: North Mankato,
Minnesota : Capstone Press, [2018] | Series: America: 50 years of change | Includes
bibliographical references and index Identifiers: LCCN 2017038578 (print) | LCCN
2017046239 (ebook) | ISBN 9781543503937 (eBook PDF) | ISBN 9781543503852
(hardcover) | ISBN 9781543503890 (pbk.) Subjects: LCSH: Protest movements—
United States—History—20th century—Juvenile literature. | Political participation—
United States-—History—20th century—Juvenile literature. | United States—Social
conditions—1960-1980—Juvenile literature. | United States—History—1961-1969—
Juvenile literature.Classification: LCC HN58 (ebook) | LCC HN58 .B675 2018 (print) |
DDC 303.48/40973--dc23 LC record available at https://lccn.loc.gov/2017038578

Editorial Credits
Michelle Bisson, editor; Russell Griesmer, designer; Svetlana Zhurkin,
media researcher; Laura Manthe, production specialist

Printed in the United States of America.
010844S18

TABLE OF CONTENTS

Thousands took part in an antiwar demonstration outside the United Nations in 1967.

SUPPORT OUR GIs-
BRING THEM
HOME NOW

STOP THE WAR NOW!

CHAPTER 1

THE 1960S: DECADE OF CHANGE

Protest has been a part of the United States since its founding. In 1773 the British government imposed an import tax on tea in its American colony. A group of patriots protested by sneaking aboard three British ships in the Boston harbor and dumping 342 chests of tea into the water. This act enraged the British and made the prospect of war with the colonies closer than ever.

Those in power have typically sought to tighten their grip on that power, often by oppressing those with less of it. Equal treatment for all is often obtained only after fierce opposition to oppression— and sometimes not even then. The 1960s were a time when protest in the United States was as fierce as it has ever been.

We can still feel the reverberations of that fight today.

CHANGING TIMES

For many Americans the beginning of the 1960s was a time of security and opportunity. The end of World War II had made the United States into the most powerful and wealthy nation on Earth. The gross national product— or GNP, a measure of a country's economy—more than doubled from $212 billion in 1945 to $503 billion in 1960. Unemployment was low, wages were rising, and the first credit cards were created. This combination gave citizens newfound ability to make large purchases of such items as houses,

The kind of "typical" American family shown on TV

cars, TV sets, refrigerators, radios, and more. Interstate highways were built all over the country, making transportation easier than ever. TV and radio commercials bubbled about toys, vacations, and other leisure products that many could afford for the first time.

It was an era of optimism, but not everyone shared equally in the advantages. During the war, women had taken many jobs while men were off

fighting. But after the war, many were laid off. Women were expected once again to lead a traditional—meaning domestic—lifestyle. Not all women were happy to find themselves confined to the life of a housewife. Those who did find work made much less money than men, often leaving them unable to earn an independent living.

Also during the war, many African Americans and other minorities had experienced greater equality than they had before. They fought and died alongside white Americans. But when they returned home, they faced continuing discrimination. They had trouble finding good jobs or housing. Racist laws prevented them from voting, earning equal pay to whites, or even using the same public facilities as whites. As much of America prospered, black America mostly remained poor and oppressed, on the outside looking in. By the 1960s African Americans were

U.S. Marines patrolled the border of Laos during the Vietnam War.

frustrated and angry that they were not sharing in America's post-war wealth.

Soon another war was beginning to cast a shadow across the country. Conflict between North Vietnam, supported by communists, and South Vietnam, supported by the U.S., had existed since shortly after World War II. But by the mid-1960s, the United States was stepping up its involvement. And an American antiwar movement began attracting more supporters who felt the country should not be involved in the conflict. When President Lyndon B. Johnson ordered bombings of North Vietnam targets in 1965, the antiwar movement became larger. It included many college students, artists, and intellectuals across the United States.

Members of the antiwar movement did not believe that the United States should be fighting the war in Vietnam. War supporters in the government said the United Sates needed to fight

Many lived in poverty in the
United States of the 1960s.

SIMMERING TENSIONS

By the mid-1960s, unease was growing in many separate American communities. African Americans and other minorities were increasingly angry at the prejudice, discrimination, and even violence they faced. They were frustrated with the slow or stopped pace of progress toward civil rights. Likewise, women were angry and frustrated at their unequal treatment. And a counterculture movement—made up largely of young, left-leaning students— was also frustrated. They questioned the values of the country's government and business leaders. They included antiwar supporters who wanted an end to the escalating Vietnam War. And all of these groups wanted a fairer economic system. Sometimes together and sometimes separately, members of these movements began to embrace protest as a method of achieving their goals.

the spread of communism and free the people of South Vietnam from the Communist forces trying to conquer them. But antiwar supporters believed the United States did not need to be involved and that they were making the fighting worse. They believed that too many Americans and Vietnamese were dying. Also, they felt the government was spending too much money on the war instead of addressing social issues such as poverty and racism.

Women, including Jeannette Rankin (center, wearing glasses), the first woman elected to Congress, marched in protest of the Vietnam War.

A Ku Klux Klan (KKK) member held a noose outside his car right before a primary election. African Americans were terrorized by the KKK after the Civil War and throughout the early years of the 20th century.

There's little doubt that the fast pace of change in the United States from World War II through the 1960s left the country ripe for reform. But to trace the birth and growth of the 1960s protests, it's helpful to go back to earlier history.

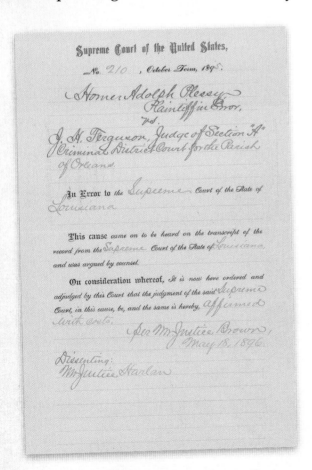

The U.S. Supreme Court's *Plessy v. Ferguson* decision turned inequality into law.

THE AFRICAN AMERICAN EXPERIENCE

Seeds of the civil rights movement of the 1960s were planted a hundred years earlier, when the Civil War ended. Soon after, a series of amendments to the U.S. Constitution granted rights to black Americans. In 1865 the 13th Amendment officially ended slavery. In 1868 the 14th Amendment officially granted citizenship to former slaves. Two years later the 15th Amendment gave black American men the right to vote. In the years right after that, some black men won election to state governments and the U.S. Congress.

But many white people resisted these

changes. They were able to deny many blacks their right to vote by passing laws establishing poll taxes (voting fees) and literacy tests for voting. Often, white people were not even asked to pay these fees or take the tests. But black people were, and without the money to pay the poll taxes, or the ability to read and write, most former slaves were turned away at the polls.

Also, some white people turned to violence to prevent blacks from claiming their rights granted under the Constitution. The Ku Klux Klan and other white supremacist organizations sprang up. They terrorized both white and black people who supported equality for blacks. Wearing hoods and masks, Klan members intimidated, beat, tortured, and murdered for the purpose of maintaining white superiority.

SEPARATE AND UNEQUAL

In 1892 a black man in New Orleans attempted to sit in a whites-only railway car. He was arrested and imprisoned. As part of a planned protest, he brought his case before the Louisiana Supreme Court, and later he brought it to the U.S. Supreme Court. The Court's ruling in the *Plessy v. Ferguson* case established that it was legal for state and local governments to treat whites and blacks as "separate but equal." Racial segregation of drinking fountains and in railway cars, buses, restaurants,

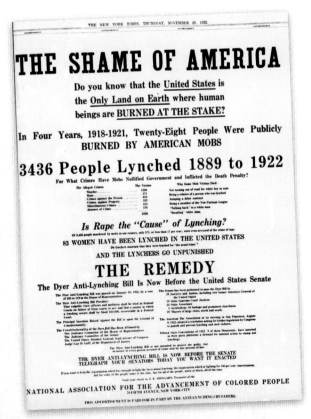

An NAACP advertisement urged passage of bill against lynching.

restrooms, parks, and schools became law throughout the South. Although these Jim Crow laws asserted that facilities would be equal, facilities for black people were almost always of far inferior quality—if they existed at all.

Discriminatory hiring and inferior schools made it hard for black Americans to make economic gains. Using separate, inferior facilities, especially in transportation, was humiliating. And, though black men legally had the right to vote, that right was often denied them through local, racially motivated laws such as literacy tests—and the threat of violence by whites. Without the vote, blacks were powerless to change things politically. Meanwhile, blacks faced open racism in many forms, including police brutality and other violence. They often feared for their safety in the presence of whites.

In 1909 a group of black and white civil rights activists formed an

Many black Americans lived in housing that was inferior to the homes built for white people.

organization to help raise awareness about—and fight back against—racism and discrimination. The National Association for the Advancement of Colored People (NAACP) started with just 60 members, but quickly grew. It fought segregation laws in court and worked to end discrimination in housing, education, employment, voting, and transportation. It also raised public awareness about lynching and other issues through its magazine, *The Crisis*. The NAACP fought for black rights on the national and local levels. Its success in changing laws, growing membership, and raising awareness about civil rights issues showed that protest could lead to real change.

The South was jolted when, in 1954, the U.S. Supreme Court ruled in *Brown v. Board of Education* that segregation in public schools was illegal. Schools were ordered to integrate, but once again many whites resisted fiercely, often violently. The most visible example happened in 1957 in Little Rock, Arkansas, where the school board ordered an all-white high school, Central High School, to integrate. Nine African American students registered and went to school the first day of classes. But the Arkansas governor ordered the Arkansas National Guard to prevent the students from entering the building. As the armed soldiers blocked the students' way, a mob of white protesters screamed obscenities, spit on the students, and threatened them. After a few weeks, President Dwight D. Eisenhower

The National Guard led nine African American students into Central High School in 1957.

persuaded the governor to remove the Guard troops, and Little Rock police escorted the students into the school through an angry mob of about 1,000 rioting white protesters. On September 24, Eisenhower sent in 1,200 members of the U.S. Army's 101st Airborne Division to protect the students and maintain order. The school was integrated.

By this time people all over the United States were becoming aware of the fight for equal rights that was growing in the South. The 1955 bus boycott in Montgomery, Alabama, had successfully led to the integration of the city's buses. Out of that protest, a new organization was formed: the Southern Christian Leadership Conference (SCLC). The leader of this Atlanta, Georgia, group was Martin Luther King Jr. He would soon emerge as one of the most important leaders of the civil rights movement in the 1960s.

BUS PROTEST

One of the most iconic civil rights protests happened five years before the dawn of the 1960s. One day in December 1955, Rosa Parks, a 42-year-old black woman from Montgomery, Alabama, was riding a segregated bus home from work. Parks refused to give up her seat to a white passenger. She was arrested and fined, but her action sparked a boycott of Montgomery buses by black riders that lasted over a year. Blacks used the buses more often than whites, and losing so many riders hurt the city financially. The boycott didn't end until the Supreme Court ordered Montgomery to integrate its buses. A new leader emerged out of the boycott, a young pastor named Martin Luther King Jr., who would become a symbol of the civil rights movement.

NEWCOMERS, NATIVES, AND POVERTY

African Americans weren't the only group that faced discrimination throughout the 19th and 20th centuries. Although the United States was founded and built by immigrants, newcomers had long been treated poorly. In the 19th century each new wave of Asian or European immigrants had access only to the least desirable jobs and housing. And Native Americans, who had been stripped of their property and rights by the earliest European settlers, also did not share in the country's prosperity.

The U.S. saw a huge influx of Hispanic immigrants during the 1950s and 1960s. Mexicans lived primarily in western states, while Puerto Ricans settled in New York's Harlem and other East Coast communities. Many were extremely poor. Because they lacked education and spoke little or no English, they were forced to take only the most

The North was segregated too. In the 1950s many Puerto Rican immigrants lived in what was dubbed Spanish Harlem.

tedious, unskilled jobs, and were unable to work their way out of poverty.

Conditions were not much better for farm workers, who were also primarily Hispanic. Migrant workers desperate for employment were exploited by farm owners. They were paid extremely low wages, and they had to pay to live in unheated, overcrowded metal shacks. These shacks typically had no indoor plumbing and no cooking facilities, and they were infested with mosquitoes.

Workers often had to pay just for a cup of water.

Similarly, Native Americans largely lived in poverty as a result of centuries of unfair treatment by the U.S. government. This included policies such as the Indian Removal Act of 1830, which relocated Native Americans from their ancestral lands to controlled reservations. Living on property controlled by the government made it hard for Native Americans to prosper. The Indian Relocation Act of 1956 further dislocated Native Americans and concentrated them in more poverty: Uprooted Native Americans moved to cities where they had little or no community support and even more extreme poverty.

Meanwhile, middle-class whites were increasingly moving to suburban neighborhoods. This left inner cities that were populated mainly by blacks, Hispanics, and other minorities with low-paying jobs—or no jobs at all. Unemployment grew, and so did other problems, such as crime and poor schools. Even as many Americans began to take notice of more direct instances of racism in the South, the dark reality of inner-city poverty went largely unnoticed and unaddressed by mainstream America. As with civil rights, it would be protest that would bring America's attention to the injustice

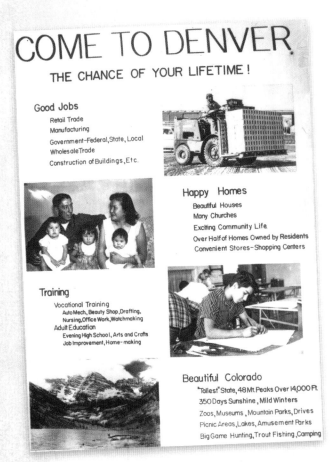

COME TO DENVER
THE CHANCE OF YOUR LIFETIME !

Good Jobs
Retail Trade
Manufacturing
Government-Federal, State, Local
Wholesale Trade
Construction of Buildings, Etc.

Happy Homes
Beautiful Houses
Many Churches
Exciting Community Life
Over Half of Homes Owned by Residents
Convenient Stores-Shopping Centers

Training
Vocational Training
Auto Mech, Beauty Shop, Drafting,
Nursing, Office Work, Watchmaking
Adult Education
Evening High School, Arts and Crafts
Job Improvement, Home-making

Beautiful Colorado
"Tallest" State, 48 Mt. Peaks Over 14,000 Ft.
350 Days Sunshine, Mild Winters
Zoos, Museums, Mountain Parks, Drives
Picnic Areas, Lakes, Amusement Parks
Big Game Hunting, Trout Fishing, Camping

An advertisement urged Native Americans to leave the reservation for employment.

of poverty. The fight by minorities in the inner cities to rise out of poverty became linked with the fight for civil rights.

THE COUNTERCULTURE MOVEMENT

Another protest movement—the counterculture movement—grew indirectly out of the relative prosperity of white Americans in the years after World War II. In the 1950s it was common for young white Americans to have better educations and earn more money than their parents had. They often bought bigger homes in the suburbs, homes that typically were built in rows and looked identical to one another. The neighborhoods felt anonymous compared to the cultural centers of the urban city, and residents felt less emphasis on community and more on simply fitting in.

But some young people felt restricted by this conformity and began to resist it. They valued individuality over conformity. Writers such as Jack Kerouac and Allen Ginsberg wrote about a life outside society's expectations—they sought openness and freedom. Rock and roll music began to capture the imagination of young people. Movie stars such as Marlon Brando and James Dean made being a rebel look cool.

In 1960 the Students for a Democratic Society (SDS) grew out of the civil rights movement. This group was founded at the University of Michigan and coined

All the houses were built to look just the same in a 1950s Long Island, New York, housing development.

the term "the New Left" for its focus on left-wing politics. The group recruited members on college campuses and advocated for more liberal policies on student issues. They were for minority admissions and free speech and against discrimination by sororities and fraternities.

By the late 1960s the counterculture had become a huge movement. Many teen boys and young men grew their hair long, and hippies dressed outlandishly as a way to assert individuality. Women let their hair go natural. Many hippies embraced drugs and alternative lifestyles such as group living or existing on what they could grow and make themselves instead of holding down a conventional job. In addition to protesting for individual freedoms such as free speech, most in the counterculture joined the fight for civil rights.

The counterculture movement included many antiwar activists. When the United States began sending troops to fight in Vietnam, TV news showed young men coming home from the war in coffins. Many soldiers who lived were severely injured and mentally scarred. These images—and the fact that many considered the war itself to be immoral—sparked massive opposition to the war by students and others throughout the U.S. When the U.S. government instituted a draft lottery to force young men into service, opposition spiked even higher.

THE WOMEN'S CAUSE

Women had been publicly fighting for equal treatment to men in the United States since at least 1848. That was the year activist Elizabeth Cady Stanton led the Woman's Rights Convention at Seneca Falls, New York. Two years later, another activist, Lucy Stone, led the National Woman's Rights Convention.

Women suffragists picketed the
White House.

In 1863 the two groups joined together
to form the Women's National Loyal
League. Its leader, Susan B. Anthony,
wrote and proposed an amendment
to the Constitution that would allow
women to vote.

In 1913 women marched for the right
to vote as President Woodrow Wilson
was about to be inaugurated. The march
provoked a violent reaction by men
opposed to women's suffrage. But the
march also attracted more attention
to the movement. Suffragists picketed

the White House in 1917. The protests
led to 218 women from 26 states being
arrested and jailed. This too helped the
movement gain influence, and in 1920
Anthony's amendment became law. At
last, women had the right to vote.

Over the next few decades, several
women's rights groups worked for equal
treatment, but they were not as active
as they were when fighting for suffrage.
During World War II, thousands of
women went to work in factories and
elsewhere, helping the country's war
effort. When these women were laid off
after the war to give their jobs to men,
they were expected to take on roles as
homemakers and mothers. Even TV
shows of the time presented men as
hardworking heads of households and
women as housewives and consumers.

In spite of these pressures, many
women found work outside the home.
In 1960 about 35 percent of women held
jobs. But they were limited in terms of

what jobs they could take. Women were commonly clerks, teachers, secretaries, and nurses because they could not get hired for jobs traditional to men, from truck drivers to lawyers to architects. Pay was poor compared to what men made, and women were often subjected to sexism on the job.

By the 1960s a new feminist movement was growing to resist gender stereotyping and the restrictive

Women worked on aircraft during World War II.

expectations put on women. These views were summarized in a 1963 book by Betty Friedan called *The Feminine Mystique*. Friedan argued, "Our culture does not permit women to accept or gratify their basic need to grow and fulfill their potentialities as human beings." Basically, women were treated as less important than men and were not allowed to find their own identity—one that was not tied to being a wife or mother. At a time when girls could not hope to grow up to be doctors, lawyers, or other professionals, the book struck a chord with many women.

THE MOVEMENT GROWS

Toward the end of the 1960s, when the civil rights and counterculture movements had gained a large following and begun to make positive changes, more movements began to embrace protest as a method of achieving change. One group was gays and lesbians.

At the time most states still had laws on the books that made homosexual acts illegal. In many cases gay men and women were barred from working for the government, and they could not serve in the military. Gays and lesbians faced open ridicule, hostility, and often physical danger from mainstream prejudiced Americans. Because of this, most homosexuals hid their sexual identity.

Gay rights organizations existed before the 1960s, but they were small and operated mostly in secret. By the end of the decade, however, gay rights activists had begun protesting on a larger scale. Their goals were to end legal discrimination against homosexuals and gain social acceptance.

Similarly concern about the environment had existed before, but it was not until the activist 1960s that a large movement began protesting to protect Earth. In 1962 biologist Rachel Carson published a book, *Silent Spring*, which detailed the harmful effects of chemical pesticides on the environment. This and other books that discussed environmental disasters and risks helped spread the word about the urgent need to protect the environment. Oil spills off the coast of California and pollution in the Great Lakes served to rally activists. In 1967 pollution in the Cuyahoga River, which flows into Lake Erie, was so bad that it caught fire. The environmental movement was concerned with pollution threats to wildlife as well as human health. Protests were aimed at raising awareness among ordinary citizens as well as to change laws.

A bird was covered in oil after an oil spill off the coast of Santa Barbara, California, in 1969.

Student sit-ins occurred
throughout the United States.

Though many of the lasting images from the protest era of the 1960s portray violence, the vast majority of protest was nonviolent. The Greensboro sit-in, an early protest in the civil rights movement, was carefully planned as a nonviolent action. The four black college students who started the protest were influenced by the nonviolent protest techniques pioneered by Mahatma Gandhi in India.

On February 1, 1960, Ezell Blair Jr., David Richmond, Franklin McCain, and Joseph McNeil went to the Woolworth's lunch counter in Greensboro, North Carolina, where only whites were allowed service. When they were denied service, they refused to give up their

Protesters marched in front of a Woolworth's in Harlem, New York, in support of those protesting segregated lunch counters in North Carolina.

seats. The police were called, but this tactic of nonviolent direct action was disarming to the police. They didn't know how to react. The local media covered the events on television.

When the lunch counter closed that

night, the students went home, but they returned the next day with more students. Within a few days about 300 young people had joined the protest. Woolworth's was unable to conduct regular business, and other local businesses were obstructed as well. By this time TV coverage had spread all over the nation, and students in other cities began to conduct their own sit-ins.

In Nashville, a group of students staged sit-ins at stores all over the city. The students were verbally harassed and sometimes physically attacked, but they remained devoted to their mission of nonviolence. Here, more than 150 students were arrested. After the home of one of their lawyers was bombed, the protest took on a new form when students spontaneously decided to march to city hall.

The small group started at the edge of Nashville, but as it got closer to city hall, more and more people joined them. By the time they reached the plaza where city hall was, the group consisted of approximately 4,000 people. Nashville mayor Ben West came out to meet the protesters, and one student, Diane Nash, asked him a question: Do you think it's wrong to discriminate against people because of their race or color?

Mayor West was moved by Nash's sincerity and the power of the protest. He admitted that he thought segregation was wrong. Shortly thereafter, Nashville became the first southern city to begin desegregating its facilities. Later that summer Greensboro also began to desegregate.

SNCC AND THE FREEDOM RIDES

In April of 1960, inspired by the success of the sit-ins, activist Ella Baker helped establish the Student Non-Violent Coordinating Committee (SNCC). Baker had been the director of Martin Luther

King Jr.'s Southern Christian Leadership Conference (SCLC), but she left that organization because she felt it was not advocating for change fast enough. SNCC catered to younger black activists who demanded radical reform.

In May 1961 SNCC joined the Freedom Rides, a series of bus trips through the South to protest the segregation of bus terminals. Freedom Riders bused through the Deep South, and at each stop, black riders tried to use "whites-only" facilities such as restrooms and lunch counters. Early in their trip, the group received little notice. But soon, white protesters began meeting the riders at their stops and brutally attacking them. On May 14 protesters threw a bomb into a Freedom Riders bus. The riders managed to escape the burning bus. Coverage of the violence, including images of the

A Freedom Riders bus was destroyed by a mob of whites in 1961.

burning bus, brought widespread attention to the state of race relations in the American South.

The Freedom Rides continued, with some riders being beaten with clubs and other weapons and many more being arrested. Hundreds of other Freedom Riders made similar journeys over the next few months, and in September the Interstate Commerce Commission issued regulations enforcing desegregation of interstate transportation.

CIVIL RIGHTS MARCHES

In spite of the progress made by the sit-ins and Freedom Rides, by late 1962 the Jim Crow laws that kept blacks "separate but equal" were still largely intact throughout the South. That's when civil rights activists, including Martin Luther King Jr., began planning a massive demonstration that would bring worldwide attention to the struggle for civil rights. Protesters would demand voting rights, equal opportunities, and an end to segregation and discrimination. The demonstration would be a march through Washington, D.C., the nation's capital.

On August 28, 1963, about 250,000 civil rights protesters marched from the Washington Monument to the Lincoln Memorial. Some of them came from hundreds of miles away to be a part of the march. They cheered, sang songs, waved signs, and, at the Lincoln Memorial, they listened to a series of civil rights leaders give speeches. The last of the speakers was King.

King delivered his prepared remarks, but he wasn't finished speaking. "I have a dream," he told the crowd, "that one day this nation will rise up and live out the true meaning of its creed: 'We hold these truths to be self-evident: that all men are created equal.'" Today, King's powerful "I Have a Dream" speech is considered one of the greatest speeches

Martin Luther King Jr. delivered his immortal "I Have a Dream" speech in 1963.

in American history.

Protesters continued to use the peaceful protest march as a powerful weapon in fighting for civil rights. In March 1965, King and others participated in a march from Selma, Alabama, to the state capitol in Montgomery. A group of 600 people began marching on Sunday, March 7, but they were soon rushed by Alabama state troopers with whips, billy clubs, and tear gas. The violence was captured on TV. The brutal scenes disturbed many Americans watching in their homes, who had not been paying attention to the level of violence facing civil rights protesters. Two days later protesters again attempted to march from Selma to Montgomery, and again they were turned back by Alabama state troopers. That same night, a group of white segregationists attacked a group of protesters and killed a young white minister named James Reeb.

By this time the marchers in Selma had the country's attention. Alabama Governor George Wallace tried to prevent another march, but President Lyndon Johnson went on TV to pledge his support for the marchers. A U.S. district court judge ordered Governor Wallace to allow the march. Now there were more than 2,000 people ready to march, and federal National Guard troops were sent in to protect them. The marchers left Selma on March 21,

and after walking nearly 12 hours a day and sleeping in fields for three nights, they reached the steps of the Capitol in Montgomery on March 25.

The public attention focused on this historic protest march, including the violence against the protesters that showed up on TV screens across the country, was credited with greatly advancing the fight for voting rights in the southern states.

RISE IN VIOLENCE

Sit-ins and marches, especially the March on Washington because it was so big, gained attention for the activist cause and resulted in some positive changes, such as the Nashville desegregation. But for many black Americans, progress was too slow. By the mid-1960s the struggle had expanded from the South to cities in the North and West.

In 1966 the radical activist Stokely

Troopers stood on the Alabama Capitol steps as marchers gathered.

Carmichael took over as chair of SNCC and began to advocate the idea of "black power." The group, which previously had adhered to the principle of nonviolence, took the more militant point of view that blacks needed to be self-reliant and defend themselves—physically if necessary—against white violence. Even before Carmichael another important voice for a more militant approach was a black Muslim activist named Malcolm X.

Then, in 1966, Oakland, California, college students Huey Newton and Bobby Seale formed the Black Panther Party. The Panthers released a 10-point program on behalf of black people that included freedom, employment, and an end to police brutality.

As the Black Panther Party grew throughout the nation, it called for an increasingly violent agenda that included killing police officers. One party member said of cops, "The only

Black Panthers protested the trial of Huey Newton.

good pig is a dead pig." With the inflammatory language came more violent action against police (though there was still far more violence by police against blacks). From 1964 to 1969, assaults on police officers in cities such as Los Angeles, Detroit, Oakland, and New York City spiked.

ANTIWAR PROTESTS

Meanwhile, Vietnam War protesters were using many of the same methods and techniques as civil rights protesters. In fact, many of the early antiwar leaders were Freedom Riders. One of the earliest antiwar demonstrations took place in Washington, D.C., on October 21, 1967. More than 100,000 protesters gathered at the Lincoln Memorial to voice their anger at the escalating war. That night, about half of them marched through the capital to the Pentagon, headquarters of the U.S. Department of Defense. Hundreds of those protesters were arrested after they clashed with U.S. marshals and soldiers.

The anti-Vietnam War demonstration in 1967 was massive, and really brought the war home.

Two years later, on October 15, 1969, an estimated 2 million Americans participated in rallies, church services, and other meetings as part of a nationwide Moratorium to End the War in Vietnam. Taking place in dozens of cities across the country, it was reported to be the biggest single-day protest in U.S. history. Boston had the largest gathering, with about 100,000 attending a speech by South Dakota Senator George McGovern.

A month later, a Moratorium March on Washington took place in the nation's capital. It began with a Thursday night March against Death, when more than 40,000 people marched silently to the White House. Each marcher, walking in single file, carried a sign with the name of a dead American soldier or a destroyed Vietnamese village. The following Saturday, November 15, more than 500,000 protesters gathered outside the White House for an antiwar

Increasing opposition to the Vietnam War led to the Moratorium to End the War in 1969.

rally and march. One of the highlights was folk singer Pete Seeger leading the crowd in John Lennon's new song "Give Peace A Chance." In between the crowd's choruses of "All we are saying . . . is give peace a chance," Seeger called out the establishment war supporters, saying "Are you listening, Nixon?" and "Are you listening, Pentagon?"

MUHAMMAD ALI: BOXER AND DRAFT PROTESTER

In 1967 heavyweight boxing champion Muhammad Ali became one of the world's most famous protesters when he refused to be drafted. He was protesting his country's participation in the Vietnam War and its treatment of black people. He famously said, "Why should they ask me to put on a uniform and go 10,000 miles from home and drop bombs and bullets on brown people in Vietnam while so-called Negro people in Louisville are treated like dogs and denied simple human rights?" Ali had much to lose with his public protest: he was convicted in court for refusing military service. He was sentenced to five years in prison and fined $10,000 for draft evasion, but remained free while his case was appealed. However, he lost his boxing license and had his world heavyweight title stripped from him. He won the case on appeal, and was allowed to return to boxing in 1970.

RIOTS

For many minorities in the inner cities, feeling trapped in lives of poverty and isolation stirred up a rage that was ready to boil over. That's exactly what happened on August 11, 1965, when a black motorist was pulled over by two white police officers in the mostly black neighborhood of Watts, in Los Angeles. A crowd gathered to watch and grew angry when they believed the police began to physically abuse the driver. The Watts residents began to riot. The riot grew, eventually covering more than 50 square miles of south central Los Angeles, with people burning buildings, looting stores, and beating whites. Rioters shot at civilians, police officers, and firefighters.

Thousands of National Guardsmen were called in and the riot was finally ended after six days. Thirty-four people had been killed, more than 1,000 had been injured, and $40 million worth of

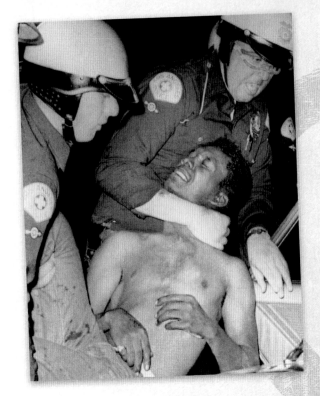

A man was forced into a police car during the Watts riots in 1965.

property had been destroyed.

The Watts riot signaled the beginning of a period of great unrest in the United States. Over the next four years, riots erupted across the country in dozens of cities. By 1971 more than 200 people died and thousands more were injured in these disturbances. Many riots were triggered by encounters between black residents and police.

Though riots were not planned, as were other forms of protest, they became a powerful symbol of the wretched poverty and living conditions that segregation and discrimination had created for minorities. Images of burning buildings on TV and in newspapers clearly showed the world that there were real problems that needed to be addressed.

Tensions in the city were high in the summer of 1968, when the Democratic Party gathered in Chicago to choose its presidential candidate. Protesters had come to town from all over the nation to advocate for many issues, mainly an end to the Vietnam War. The antiwar candidate, Minnesota Senator Eugene McCarthy, had a huge following among young voters, especially the protesters. Vice President Hubert Humphrey was considered the establishment choice. When Humphrey won the nod as the Democratic candidate, protesters felt as if he'd been chosen by the party bosses rather than the actual voters.

As a result, thousands rioted in the streets outside the convention hall. Richard J. Daley, the mayor of Chicago, had called in 12,000 police officers and 15,000 state and federal troops to control the mob. When rioting broke out, many protesters were severely beaten and teargassed, as were members of the news media and doctors who had come to help.

The following year in New York City, a series of riots helped launch the gay rights movement—which later evolved to become a national LGBTQ rights movement. The Stonewall riots began early in the morning of June 28, 1969,

Police spray antiwar demonstrators with mace at the National Democratic Convention in 1968.

when a small group of customers at the popular Greenwich Village gay bar, the Stonewall Inn, began arguing with police officers who were arresting employees and clients at the bar. Although the police said they were arresting people for breaking laws such as serving liquor without a license, the protesters felt that the bar had been targeted because it was a known gay bar. Soon neighborhood residents joined in the riot, throwing bottles and shouting "Gay power!" at the police.

Police eventually beat the crowd away but the next night more than 1,000 protesters returned and riots continued. The Stonewall riots went on for several more days and jumpstarted serious discussions of gay rights in New York City and around the country.

STRIKES

Labor strikes (when employees walk off the job or refuse to work) are another common form of protest. By the 1930s the organized labor movement was regularly using strikes to gain better pay and working conditions in a wide range of industries. And by the 1960s migrant workers—who came to the United States from other countries and often worked illegally for very low pay and under poor conditions—began using labor strikes to fight for their rights.

One of the most successful migrant labor strikes was the 1965 Delano grape strike, when Filipino American grape workers walked out on strike against California grape growers. In the past big agricultural businesses had been able

The strike against the California grape growers was ultimately successful.

to squash strikes by migrant workers, in part by pitting one community of migrant workers against another. But this time, the Filipino workers asked Cesar Chavez, a leader of the Hispanic labor movement, to join their strike. He did, after asking the strikers to promise to be nonviolent. The strike lasted for more than five years. At one point Chavez himself fasted for 25 days to ensure strikers honored their commitment to nonviolence. But ultimately the strike was successful in earning better working conditions for grape growers.

Not all protest strikes are labor strikes. In 1970 nearly 4 million student strikers shut down colleges and high schools across the United States as part of antiwar protests. Throughout the 1960s students had been active in the antiwar movement, and when President Richard Nixon announced an expansion of the Vietnam War on April 30, 1970,

thousands of students protested across the country. A few days later, National Guard members shot and killed four students at a protest at Kent State University in Ohio.

This violent reaction from the federal troops spurred some of the previously peaceful protesters to turn to violence. Soon students had burned or bombed nearly 30 Reserve Officer Training Corps (ROTC) offices on campuses across the country. By the next day the U.S. experienced its only mass student strike. Nearly 450 colleges and high schools were temporarily shut down by the 4 million strikers. Media coverage

Tear gas was used on antiwar protesters at Kent State. Soon after, four students were killed by National Guardsmen.

of the strikers—and of the Kent State shootings in particular—led to increased national questioning of the United States' involvement in Vietnam.

POPULAR CULTURE

One important goal of protest is to raise awareness about injustice and inspire people to stand up against it. When a large number of people demand change it makes that change much more likely to happen. And one way to spread the word is through popular media. In the 1960s, before the Internet made global communication as easy as a click, two of the most commonly used media were music and books. An inspiring political song could and did galvanize masses of young people.

Singers of the civil rights movement included the SNCC Freedom Singers, and folk singers Pete Seeger, Guy Carawan, and Len Chandler. Activist Fannie Lou Hamer was known for singing spiritual songs such as "This Little Light of Mine" and "Go Tell It on the Mountain." Bob Dylan was one of the most effective protest singers of that time (and of any time). He recorded many popular protest songs, but the most important may have been his first, "Blowin' in the Wind." The song captures the discontent of the era by asking questions about the morality of war and other big issues of the counterculture movement.

Other popular protest songs included "Fortunate Son" by Creedence Clearwater Revival. The song's writer, John Fogerty, saw that many in the country, especially politicians and the elite of society, had little respect for the soldiers who, like him, had served in the military. "Fortunate Son" was his angry response to a country where the rich and powerful waged war and the poor and powerless were forced to fight it.

Folk singers Joan Baez and Bob Dylan were leading voices in the protest movement.

President Lyndon Johnson signed
the Civil Rights Act into law in 1964.

The fight for social justice continued after the end of the protest-heavy 1960s. Those who had protested for civil rights, women's rights, gay rights, or in other struggles against injustice had not met all their goals by the dawn of the 1970s. Nevertheless, there were landmark advancements and accomplishments by each of those movements in the late 1950s and 1960s that changed the lives of many Americans.

CIVIL RIGHTS ACCOMPLISHMENTS

The civil rights protests of the 1950s and 1960s woke up many Americans to the injustices suffered by black Americans. Even for people who didn't participate, the powerful images of marches, sit-ins, and—maybe, most starkly—violence against protesters left their mark.

One of the most important of these marks was not a law or granted right. It was simply a change in the way white America looked at black America. Before this period, popular explanations for why black people lived in poverty cast the blame on black people themselves. But the civil rights movement made it clear that institutional racism was the main reason for inequality. During the summer of 1967, while riots were rocking American cities, President Johnson created the National Advisory Commission on Civil Disorders. The commission, which came to be known as the Kerner Commission after its chairman, Illinois Governor Otto Kerner, was given the job of explaining three basic questions: "What happened? Why did it happen? What can be done to prevent it from happening again and again?" The Kerner Commission's report spelled out quite clearly that racism had created black poverty. It said, "White society created it, white institutions maintain it, and white society condones it."

Protest also led directly and indirectly to federal laws aimed at dismantling racial injustices that had become interwoven into American society. While these laws did not end racism, discrimination, or unequal treatment, they are considered landmark achievements of the civil rights movement.

The first of these laws was the Civil Rights Act of 1957. In fact, this was the first civil rights law passed by Congress

President Johnson formed the Kerner Commission to explore the connection between racism and poverty.

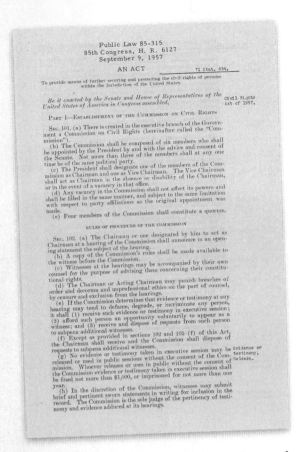

The 1957 Civil Rights Act is on display at the Library of Congress in Washington, D.C.

in 82 years. The act aimed to increase the number of African Americans who voted. Although the 15th Amendment had granted black Americans the right to vote in 1870, by 1957 only 20 percent of blacks were voting. They were systematically kept from voting by discriminatory policies such as poll taxes and literacy requirements—and by the outright discrimination of poll workers.

Because of the ongoing racism of many Americans, it was considered a major accomplishment that the 1957 Act was passed by Congress and signed by President Eisenhower. But the final version of the law was considered more symbolic than effective in increasing the number of black voters. In order to get enough support from more conservative members of Congress to get the bill passed, many compromises had been made to weaken the bill. For instance, in the final law, it was illegal for any person to get in the way of anybody's right to vote, but in reality anybody accused of that crime in a southern state would not be convicted by an all-white jury. Some leaders of the civil rights movement said they felt that because this act was so weak and difficult to enforce, it was worse than not having any law. But most agreed that it was an important first step in civil rights legislation, and it paved the way for stronger laws passed in the 1960s.

The Civil Rights Act of 1964 greatly expanded on the promise of the 1957 law. It aimed to protect not just voting rights but also employment and housing rights. It banned discrimination based on "race, color, religion, sex or national origin" in employment practices and public accommodations. This meant that blacks and other minorities could not be denied service based on the color of their skin at any public place, including courthouses, swimming pools, parks, restaurants, theaters, sports arenas, and hotels.

The act also prohibited the use of federal money for any discriminatory programs. And it included two additions that helped enforce it. First, it allowed the U.S. attorney general to file lawsuits to enforce the new law. Second, it overruled state and local laws that allowed discrimination.

The Voting Rights Act of 1965, a third piece of civil rights legislation, was a direct result of the Selma voting rights marches. Eight days after the first Selma march, President Johnson gave a speech to Congress urging its members to support the voting rights bill they would soon be voting on. He said, "What happened in Selma is part of a far larger movement which reaches into every section and state of America

. . . because it is not just Negroes, but really it is all of us, who must overcome the crippling legacy of bigotry and injustice. And we shall overcome."

The president was directly quoting protesters who chanted "We shall overcome" as he entered the U.S. Capitol to deliver the speech. Since Johnson had not always had a strong record of supporting civil rights, the protesters were skeptical of him. So when he included those three words in his speech, it had a powerful effect on civil rights protesters. Aides to King, who were watching the televised speech with him, said it was the first time they had ever seen King cry.

Congress did pass the bill. The Civil Rights Act of 1965 prohibited poll taxes, literacy tests, and other forms of voter registration discrimination. It also allowed federal agents to oversee voter registration in states where those practices had been in place. Most importantly, black Americans who had been prevented from registering to vote would now have a jury of their peers—including black men and women—to hear their case of voter discrimination.

These legislative accomplishments were in part brought about by the protest actions of the 1950s and 1960s. They were significant, but they did not mean that black Americans had achieved equality. By the end of the 1960s it was still common for black families to live in segregated, less desirable parts of cities or towns. It was common for them to have less access to good schools, health care, and opportunities for employment. In 1970 black men were earning on average about 60 percent of what white men earned and the unemployment rate for blacks was more than twice as high than it was for whites.

WAR ON POVERTY

At the same time that the federal government was responding to racial unrest and protests with landmark civil rights legislation, President Johnson was also declaring what he dubbed a War on Poverty. It aimed to reduce the crippling impact of poverty on so many Americans. In the early 1960s the official U.S. poverty rate was 19 percent. As he announced in his 1964 State of the Union speech, "Our aim is not only to relieve the symptoms of poverty, but to cure it and, above all, to prevent it."

The War on Poverty included four major laws. The largest was the Economic Opportunity Act of 1964, which created programs for low-income youth. These jobs included Job Corps, the VISTA program, and the federal work-study program. It also created the White House Office of Economic Opportunity, which was dedicated to fighting the war on poverty. This office soon created the Head Start program for low-income preschool-age children.

President Johnson spoke to a man in Appalachia as he traveled around the country to promote his War on Poverty.

Another law, the Social Security Amendments of 1965, created Medicare and Medicaid and expanded Social Security benefits for retirees, widows, people with disabilities, and other low-income individuals. The Food Stamp Act of 1964 made the test food stamp program permanent. The Elementary and Secondary Education Act of 1965 provided extra education funding to school districts with large proportions of low-income families.

Although these laws were not aimed directly at any one minority group, they benefited nearly all groups with large concentrations of people living in poverty.

WOMEN'S RIGHTS ACCOMPLISHMENTS

Women benefited from civil rights legislation passed in the 1960s. The Civil Rights Act of 1964 and other civil rights laws banned discrimination on the basis of sex as well as race, religion, and other factors. The Equal Pay Act of 1963 was aimed specifically at protecting women's rights. It banned employers from paying women less than men for the same work. In *Griswold v. Connecticut*, in 1965, the Supreme Court struck down a law restricting access to contraception for married couples. In 1967 Johnson included women on the list of classes that employers could not discriminate against under affirmative action laws.

Judging from these laws and even television sitcoms like *That Girl*—the first show to feature a young, single, career-minded woman, premiering in 1966—it seemed that women's rights had been achieved. And yet women did not feel that way. Women generally were still expected to choose a family over a career. And when they did have a job, they were usually paid less and promoted less that their male counterparts. And they still had to do all the housework and childcare. On August 26, 1970—the 50th anniversary of women's suffrage—the Women's Strike for Equality took place in more than 90 cities across the country.

LGBTQ RIGHTS ACCOMPLISHMENTS

Although the Stonewall riots of 1969 had firmly launched the gay rights movement, it would take a long line of lawsuits and judicial actions to advance gay rights over the following half century. However, the Stonewall protests did inspire gay people throughout the country to advocate for rights. Within two years of the riots, gay rights groups had been started in nearly every major city in the United States. And on the first anniversary of the Stonewall riots, the first gay pride parades in U.S. history took place in Los Angeles, Chicago, San Francisco, and near the Stonewall Inn in New York.

OTHER MOVEMENTS

Cesar Chavez and his United Farm Workers strikes succeeded in getting higher wages and better conditions for farm workers throughout the American West. But they did more than that. As millions of Americans stopped eating grapes in solidarity with the workers, they saw that ordinary people could make a real difference in helping the poor and underpaid.

Other workers also went on strike for

Many people marched in the Gay and Lesbian Pride Parade in 1970.

better wages and working conditions. From 1967 to 1974, there were an average of 5,200 strikes per year, many of them successful.

The success of the environmental movement can be seen in the fact that Congress enacted the National Environmental Act in 1970. The act strengthened the regulation of environmental health hazards and the use of natural resources. Also in 1970, Wisconsin Senator Gaylord Nelson proposed a national teach-in on the environment, and on April 22, 1970, 20 million Americans participated in rallies for a healthy, sustainable environment. It was the first Earth Day. In the coming years, Congress would pass many more laws to protect the environment, including the Clean Air Act and the Clean Water Act, which established national air-quality and water-quality standards.

Citizens began to work to conserve natural resources and use and develop alternative, cleaner forms of energy. They demanded strict regulation of toxins and increased awareness of the interconnectedness and interdependency of all life. By the late 1970s, much of the environmental movement's agenda had entered mainstream politics, even though there was still much work to do.

Kids wore antipollution masks on Earth Day, 1970, in New York City.

Occupy Wall Street formed in 2011 to protest economic injustice.

In some important ways, a lot has changed for the better since the 1960s. New laws created legal supports for causes and barriers to discrimination. The fierce public discussion created an atmosphere in which more people understood the oppression and injustice that some in the country suffered. Polls showed that white people's feelings toward black people changed during the 1960s. In 1958 the number of whites who said they were willing to vote for a black president was 38 percent. In 1965 that number had risen to 59 percent, and by 1970 it was 70 percent. Most people were in favor of social programs to help the poor, and most favored integrated neighborhoods. Outwardly racist behavior, which had been common a decade earlier, had become socially unacceptable.

But, by important economic measures, little progress—if any—has been made. African Americans still have a much harder time than white Americans finding work. In 1972 the unemployment rate for blacks was 2.04 times what it was for whites. In 2013 the ratio had barely budged: it was 2.02. In 2016 26 percent of black households were "food insecure," or hungry, including 30 percent of black children.

In the United States, black communities are policed far more intensely than white ones. Black people are incarcerated six times more often

Thousands showed up at a job fair in the middle of the 2009 recession.

In February 2012 a 17-year-old African American high school student named Trayvon Martin was walking in a Florida neighborhood on his way home from a convenience store. A resident of the area, George Zimmerman, shot and killed him. Though Zimmerman was charged with murder, he claimed that Martin had attacked him, and he was acquitted.

In the wake of the acquittal, when many media stories focused on criticizing Martin instead of his killer, three activists started the #blacklivesmatter hashtag on social media. It was an assertion that racism is still a powerful force in the United States. Two years later, in August 2014, another unarmed black teen was killed, this time by a police officer. Michael Brown was shot in Ferguson, Missouri, a community that had endured harsh

than whites, and police brutality continues to be a problem for black Americans. For one example of this, the Department of Justice conducted an investigation of the Philadelphia Police Department from 2007 to 2013. It found that 80 percent of the people Philadelphia cops had shot were African American, though the city's population is less than 50 percent black. Worst of all, white cops are still likely to face no punishment for killing.

economic conditions and intense policing for years. To add insult to injury, police left Brown's body in the street for more than four hours and wouldn't let his family near.

That night a protest broke out in Ferguson. The police responded to the protest with tanks, machine guns, tear gas, and rubber bullets. Over the next several days, the protest turned into a riot and police arrested 172 people. At the same time, more protests and riots occurred in other cities throughout the country. The scene in Ferguson was a breaking point for many black citizens who felt oppressed by the police. They had witnessed too many black men being killed by police officers without the police being brought to account.

As one protester said, "We all had the same pain and anger about this. We all came together that day. . . . They're killing us, and it's not right."

The movement to raise awareness about police brutality toward African Americans came together under the #blacklivesmatter banner.

Black Lives Matter formed as a protest against police brutality toward young black men.

In the months and years that followed Brown's death, many more African Americans have been killed by police. With cell phone cameras and social media, regular citizens have brought their protest to the Internet as a way to spread the word when mainstream media is not fast enough to tell the story the minute it occurs.

Protests are only effective if the message gets out. That's why social media can be such a powerful tool. Celebrities can also get out the message fast. During the 2016 NFL football season, San Francisco 49ers quarterback Colin Kaepernick knelt before every game during the national anthem instead of standing. He was protesting the killing of black men by police. His action was discussed at length throughout the nation. In 2017 the protest spread across the entire league. It was condemned by President Trump but applauded by many others.

WORLD TRADE ORGANIZATION AND THE OCCUPY MOVEMENT

In 1999 the World Trade Organization (WTO), which regulates international trade, had a conference in Seattle, Washington. The group planned to set a global trade-negotiation agenda for the next millennium. But many people saw a threat looming in the increasing globalization. They felt that many American jobs were going to less expensive workers in other countries

A police officer in Seattle asked demonstrators to move or they would be pepper sprayed.

and looser regulation posed a danger to the health and safety of the environment and people everywhere.

Labor unions, environmental groups, student groups, and others planned a massive protest of the conference. On November 28, when members of the WTO began to arrive in Seattle, several hundred people protested downtown. In the following days, the protests grew to 40,000 people. Many were self-described anarchists who smashed windows, spray-painted graffiti, and damaged police cars. Police in riot gear responded and many protesters were arrested. But WTO negotiations broke down, marking a victory for the protesters.

Over the next decade, the United States fell into a recession caused largely by big banks providing housing loans to people who couldn't afford them. Various other factors contributed to a widening income gap, where the rich were getting richer and the poor were getting poorer. The middle class was shrinking. That, combined with perceived corporate greed and corporate influence on government, led to the feeling that regular people were economically disadvantaged and oppressed by the wealthiest Americans.

On September 17, 2011, protesters occupied a park on Wall Street in New York City's financial district. The occupation got widespread coverage and grew quickly, not only in New York but worldwide. The movement's slogan, "We are the 99%," referred to the fact that the wealthiest 1 percent of Americans held a hugely unbalanced share of money, and the feeling that this gave the 1 percent too much power over the rest of the nation.

Over the following weeks and months, the movement grew to nearly 1,000 cities worldwide, bringing new attention to the issue of economic inequality and corporate influence.

These issues are now a major part of political discussion in the U.S.

STANDING ROCK

In early 2016 plans were announced for the creation of the Dakota Access pipeline, a pipeline that would pump oil from oil fields in western North Dakota to southern Illinois. The pipeline would go under the Missouri and Mississippi rivers, posing a threat to clean drinking water. It would also be built under the sacred burial grounds of the Standing Rock Indian Reservation.

To prevent construction of the pipeline, a group of Standing Rock natives began to camp in the construction area, and soon people from all over North America traveled to North and South Dakota to join the protest. Thousands of people occupied the camp and clashed with police who tried to remove them. Police used attack dogs to clear one area. On other occasions, they shot protesters with water cannons during freezing winter weather.

Wind, snow, and freezing-cold weather did not deter the protesters at Standing Rock.

The protests, which brought international attention to the issue, were successful in temporarily postponing construction of the pipeline. But in January 2017 President Donald J. Trump ordered construction to continue.

ELECTION OF DONALD TRUMP

In November 2016 Republican Donald Trump was elected president. Many were unhappy with his election, and it sparked a flurry of new protest action. During his campaign Trump had promised to strengthen the economy. He also promised to bar Muslims from entering the United States. He promised to roll back laws that protected immigrants and women. He said he did not believe in global climate change and promised to eliminate or change laws that protected the environment. He was caught on audio admitting to sexually assaulting women.

After his inauguration on January 20, 2017, people all over the country protested. On January 21 millions of women and men participated in the Women's March to advocate for women's rights as well as a host of other causes, including immigration rights, LGBTQ rights, environmental stewardship, and maintaining healthcare reform.

Days later, when President Trump signed an executive order banning travel from seven majority Muslim countries, thousands of people spontaneously protested against the ban at airports all over the country and the world.

On April 22—Earth Day—more than 600 cities held marches advocating for scientific research and in opposition to President Trump's policies and budget cuts at the Environmental Protection Agency and other government departments. It was estimated that a million people worldwide took part in a March for Science.

POPULAR CULTURE

As in the 1960s, popular culture is still a powerful tool for change. Protest songs are perhaps more popular than ever, and they are being produced by a diverse group of artists. Examples include "Alright" by Kendrick Lamar, "We the People" by A Tribe Called Quest, "Born Free" by MIA, "Freedom" by Beyonce, and "Standing in the Way of Control" by Gossip.

THE FIGHT GOES ON

Racism, while less obvious than it was in the 1950s, remains a very real problem in the United States today. Police brutality wreaks havoc on African American communities. Economic inequality remains a stark reality. The top 1 percent of Americans earn about $1.3 million a year—about 20 percent of all U.S. income—while the bottom 50 percent earn about $16,000. The figure for the bottom 50 percent hasn't changed since 1980.

For those who protest against injustice, these are not encouraging thoughts. After all this time, there is still a grave need to advocate for better housing, wages, education, and policing for minorities and the poor. And as always, the backlash against protest is strong: those with power, and the politically conservative, typically feel strong opposition to the fight for change. They criticize those who protest as unpatriotic and ungrateful for what they have. They will fight change with legal and sometimes physical means.

But the protest movement remains strong. In spite of the opposition, many people are still willing to fight for what they feel is right. They have not given up fighting for better lives.

Thousands took part in the Women's March in
Washington, D.C., on January 21, 2017.

GLOSSARY

affirmative action—an active effort to improve employment, educational opportunities, or other needs for disadvantaged groups

boycott—when people refuse to buy or use something or refuse to deal with a person or organization as a way of protesting

civil rights—basic human rights that pertain to individual freedom

counterculture—subculture whose values and behaviors are in stark contrast to the mainstream

discrimination—unfair treatment of a person or group, often because of race, religion, gender, sexual preference, or age

establishment—authorities or others who are formally in charge and hold power

integrate—bring together different parts; in the context of civil rights, to make opportunities and institutions such as school equally available to all races

Jim Crow—state and local laws that enforced racial segregation in the Southern United States

LGBTQ—initials that stand for lesbian, gay, bisexual, transgender, and questioning

migrant worker—laborer who travels to follow seasonal work

segregation—practice of separating people of different races, income classes, or ethnic groups

sit-in—when people occupy a building or area as a way of protesting

strike—when people stop work or refuse to do something as a way of protesting; a strike can hinder a business's ability to operate and force it to negotiate with protesters

suffrage—the right to vote

READ MORE

Adichie, Chimamanda Ngozi. *We Should All Be Feminists.* New York: Anchor Books, 2015.

Burgan, Michael. *Death at Kent State: How a Photograph Brought the Vietnam War Home to America.* North Mankato, Minn.: Compass Point Books, 2016.

Coates, Ta-Nehisi. *Between the World and Me.* New York: Spiegel & Grau, 2015.

Cummings, Judy Dodge. *Rebels & Revolutions: Real Tales of Radical Change in America.* Atlanta: Peachtree Press, 2017.

Edwards, Sue Bradford, and Duchess Harris. *Black Lives Matter.* Minneapolis: Essential Books, 2016.

Thompson, Laurie Ann. *Changemaker: How to Start Something that Matters.* New York: Simon Pulse/Beyond Words, 2014.

CRITICAL THINKING QUESTIONS

1. Consider the ways that white people reacted to black protests in the 1960s and how they react today. What differences and similarities do you see? Why do you think that is?

2. Many protesters of the 1960s used their actions to advocate for several different reforms. For example, Muhammad Ali's draft refusal was in protest of both the Vietnam War and the unequal treatment of blacks. Are some of today's protesters addressing separate but related issues? How?

3. Sometimes protesting for what you believe in can be dangerous. What is something you believe strongly in? Would you risk your safety to fight for it? Why or why not?

4. The Internet and especially social media have changed the way we communicate today. How has it affected protest movements? Do you think the changes help or hurt causes? Why?

INTERNET SITES

Use FactHound to find internet sites related to this book.

Visit *www.facthound.com*

Just type in 9781543503852 and go.

ABOUT THE AUTHOR

Eric Braun writes fiction and nonfiction for kids, teens,
and adults on many topics. Recently, one of his books
was launched into space to be read for kids on Earth
by an astronaut on the International Space Station.
He lives in Minneapolis with his wife, sons, and dog, Willis.

INDEX